REFRESH, REVIVE AND RESTORE

BY

DR. RUSS MOYER

Unless otherwise noted, all scripture references are from T*he New King James Version of the Bible*, copyright © 1979, 1980, 1982, by Thomas Nelson, Inc., Nashville, TN. References marked KJV are taken from *The Holy Bible, King James Version*, public domain. References marked NIV are from *The Holy Bible, New International Version*, copyright © 1973, 1978, 1984 by International Bible Society, Colorado Springs, Colorado. References marked NLT are from *The Holy Bible, New Living Translation*, copyright © 1996, 2004, 2007 by Tyndale House Foundation. Used by permission of Tyndale House Publishers, Inc., Carol Stream, Illinois. References marked ESV are from the *The Holy Bible, English Standard Version*, copyright © 2001 by Crossway Bibles, a publishing ministry of Good News Publishers.

Published by:

McDougal & Associates
18896 Greenwell Springs Road
Greenwell Springs, LA 70739
www.thepublishedword.com

McDougal & Associates is an organization dedicated to the spreading of the Gospel of the Lord Jesus Christ to as many people as possible in the shortest time possible.

ISBN: 978-1-950398-84-3

Printed on demand in the U.S., the U.K., Australia and the EAU
For Worldwide Distribution

Presented To:

_____

By:

_____

On:

_____

Message:

_____

_____

_____

_____

Content

Foreword by Mave Moyer

With long life I will satisfy him. Psalm 91:16

As believers of God's Word and followers of Jesus, we have been promised that God will fulfill ALL of our days and satisfy us with long life. We do not have to slowly deteriorate in our mind and body or suffer from age-related ailments, and end up living under the care of others. We also don't have to die young. We can fulfill the call of God on our lives and finish well. I personally had to trust in and believe this as I walked by faith with my hubby through one of the most difficult few years of our lives.

Not just once did death come knocking, but twice. As we pressed into the truth that God was not finished with Russ yet, we made a decision that, in spite of how it looked or seemed, we knew God was behind the scenes, He knew all the devil's schemes, and He was greater than anything the enemy could try!

I had to trust that God would be faithful and true and He would do what He said He would do. Through this season of struggle, we had to exercise unshakable faith, not based on personal merits and accomplishments, but firmly planted in a personal relationship with Jesus and divine confidence in the love of God.

The enemy would like to take us all out, cut our lives short, and disappoint us, keeping us from walking out our God-given call. But the devil can never stop the plan of God. He might hinder or put up a roadblock or two, but he can never thwart the plan of God for me or for you.

In this book, Russ takes you with him on his personal journey through the valley of the shadow of death and then through his personal season of "being pressed" and pressing into God and being refreshed, revived, and restored. The Word of God has promised us long life, strength, and health for all our days. We can renew our youth like the eagle, and we can live long and strong. The joy of living a Christ-centered and faith-focused life is that it no longer depends on outward circumstances.

As we grow older, we accept that there are some things we may no longer do, but instead of wasting time mourning that fact, we rejoice in the things we are still called and empowered by God to do. Jesus said that when we lose our life for His sake, then we truly find it. Rather than constantly struggling to recapture our youth, we, as believers, can trust God to renew it and give us the power to accomplish the things He has ordained for us.

The cry that is on God's heart today is for total transformation. He is calling out to all of us … to change. It's a time of deep calling unto deep. Let us commit to His plan and take hold of His hand. Let's find His heart and vision for us and for our generation, so that He can take us deeper and higher in the things of the Spirit. In this special place with Him, we are assured of His commitment to us and His covenant with us. He will never leave or forsake us.

In this heartfelt account, Russ shares how he was refreshed, revived, and restored naturally, physically, spiritually, emotionally, financially, and relationally. We can trust that this is God's heart for every one of us. He wants to give us a deep understanding of our sonship and inheritance. God is interested in ALL things pertaining to you and me.

This prophetic book and account will reveal to us God in His goodness, God in His grace, God the Healer, God the Restorer, and the resurrection life. He is the God who takes us from death to life in every area, as we yield to Him and His plan.

Our destiny and legacy are not found in the things of this world. We are not held in bondage by human perspectives or by the minds and thoughts of men. God wants to take us higher and deeper and give us a Kingdom understanding and Kingdom view, a supernatural look through His eyes, the eyes of the King of Kings and the Lord of Lords. He is the great "I AM" and the one who does all things for our good and His glory. Let Him do all that He needs to do in you, so that you can arise and be everything He called you to be!

I beseech you therefore, brethren, by the mercies of God, that you present your bodies a living sacrifice, holy, acceptable to God, which is your reasonable service. And do not be conformed to this world, but be transformed by the renewing of your mind, that you may prove what is that good and acceptable and perfect will of God.

Romans 12:1-2, KJV

Mave Moyer

Repent therefore and be converted, that your sins may be blotted out, so that times of refreshing may come from the presence of the Lord, and that He may send Jesus Christ, who was preached to you before, whom heaven must receive until the times of restoration of all things, which God has spoken by the mouth of all His holy prophets since the world began.
—Acts 3:19-21

Introduction

*Prepare ye the way of the LORD, make straight
in the desert a highway for our God.*
Isaiah 40:3, KJV

As I write this, I'm sitting in my home office
in Canada, reflecting on the goodness of God.
I'm so excited about this wonderful moment
in time. At the same time, I'm also troubled
that many well-meaning believers are being
caught up in all the things that are happening
around the world.

There is no shortage of voices in our world.
The Bible tells us this in 1 Corinthians 14:10,
and, it says, all of them have a significance.
You and I, who have been marked with destiny in this generation and moment, must
listen closely, even as John the Revelator did,

laying our head on the bosom of the Lord Jesus and listening to His heartbeat.

God's heart is crying out to this generation, to you and me, not just to one or two, but to many. There is an Elijah cry going forth to prepare the way. There is a great cry for intimacy and relationship, first and foremost, with God Himself. There is a love cry on God's heart for His Bride to prepare herself for the great wedding day. There is a cry for leaders to be led by the Spirit and to lead in the Spirit with honor, character, integrity, and love.

There is a cry on God's heart for us to walk in His footsteps. There is a cry that's echoing throughout all of His creation with hope and expectation that the sons and daughters of God will manifest in hope, healing, and maturity.

There is a cry on the heart of God that is beckoning His Church to break out of the four walls of a building and become an active and essential force in bringing healing, hope, refreshing, revival, and restoration to our families, our communities, and our nations.

As I look ahead with great hope and expectation, I can't help but look back over the last seven or eight years with great thankfulness and joy for all that God has done in my own life. In the midst of great adversity, facing death and disaster, I was drinking from the wellsprings of life, tasting of the goodness of God, and experiencing His mercy and grace in new and unusual ways.

What an incredible season it has been going through my own wilderness and valley experience, while getting to know the Lord and different aspects of His heart and personality in a much greater measure! Just as Paul cried out to know God in the power of His resurrection in the midst of his personal suffering, I, too, cried out, and as He has throughout my life, over and over again, He proved Himself, His love, and His faithfulness. He is an awesome God, and there are no words in any language that are sufficient to describe Him.

Throughout this journey, the Lord has provided divine appointments, destiny encounters, friends, family, prophetic words, dreams, visions, and confirmations in the Spirit. There is not even a shadow of a doubt that He is who He says He is, and He can and will do everything

He says He will do. He is worthy of all honor, worthy of all praise.

In this book, I want to ask and answer some questions that are crucial these days, especially to those of us who know Jesus as Lord and Savior, questions like:

WHAT IS HE DOING?
WHAT DOES HE WANT ME TO DO?
WHO AM I?
OTHER "WHYS" AND "WHAT FORS"
OF MODERN LIFE.

The great cry that is on God's heart is deep unto deep. Let us take hold of His hand, His heart, and His vision for us and for our generation, so that He can take us deeper and higher in the things of the Spirit.

God has refreshed, revived, and restored me naturally, physically, spiritually, emotionally, financially, and relationally. That is His heart for every one of us, the Remnant, the Bride, the world changers, the history makers. For both the up and out and the down and out, He wants to give us a fresh revelation of our sonship, our inheritance, our destiny, and our legacy, not from the perspective of the world or the minds and thoughts of men. He wants to take us higher and give us a Kingdom view through His eyes, the eyes of the very King of Glory.

Somewhere near the beginning of this experience, the Lord asked me to take a walk with Him, and He has done that many times in my life. It was a prophetic walk, a walk through times and seasons, a walk of faith, and I was unsure of where I was going to end up. Each time it seemed like my life was wildly spinning in the midst of chaos, anarchy, and uncertainty. I knew my only hope was to put my hand in His and to walk down the road called "change."

As I did this, the Lord said, "Let's take a walk down to 'the potters house.'" I had taken that walk before, many times, with a broken heart, my life in pieces, everything scattered and undone, promises unfulfilled, not knowing how I had gotten there or even where I was going next.

In the midst of the echoes of darkness, I knew He was my only Hope and my only true Light. I just wanted to hold on to His hand with all my heart. Even that, sometimes, was not enough. All I had was the blessed assurance of knowing that He had hold of me. That is the walk of faith.

So, come now. Let's you and I take a little walk together. Let's give God all the glory, all the honor, and all the praise. He is Wonderful, the Counselor, the Spirit of Truth, the King of Kings, and the Lord of Lords. He is the Alpha and the Omega. He knows the beginning from the end. He is, He was, and He is to come.

You and I can overcome the issues of life by the word of our testimony and the blood of the lamb. May the Lord bless you and keep you, as we walk together. Yield to Him in this new and beautiful season, so that you, too, can be refreshed, revived, and restored.

—*Russ Moyer*
President of Eagle Worldwide Ministries
U.S. and Canada

Chapter 1

Refresh, Revive, and Restore

Wilt thou not revive us again: that thy people may rejoice in thee? Psalm 85:6, KJV

Revival is on my heart. Revival is in the air. Revival seems to be everywhere right now … but only if you have eyes to see and ears to hear. True, in the natural, things look rather dismal, but I'm excited because I believe we are set up for a miracle, set up for a great move of the Spirit of God. I believe we have just stepped over the threshold into a brand new season, and we are standing on the brink of a breakthrough, on the brink of a miracle, on the brink of the greatest move of the Spirit and the greatest harvest of souls in all of history. I also believe we are the generation marked with destiny to prepare the way for the Second Coming of Christ. That's why I'm so "pumped."

I've tasted of revival and drank from the river of God many times in the last twenty-five plus years, so I'm pretty much spoiled and not interested in what we know as the regular or normal Sunday go-to-meeting church. I am convinced that there is only one kind of real revival, and that's revival glory.

What is revival glory? That's when the presence and power of God is manifested, not just His omnipresence (for God is everywhere at all times), but the life-changing presence where God just shows up and takes over. This is the glory realm where everything and anything is possible.

That's what we need, for we are not changed from meeting to meeting or service to service, but from glory to glory:

> *Now the Lord is the Spirit; and where the Spirit of the Lord is, there is liberty. But we all, with unveiled face, beholding as in a mirror the glory of the Lord, are being transformed into the same image from glory to glory, just as by the Spirit of the Lord.* 2 Corinthians 3:17-18

Some people say, "There isn't any mention of revival in the Scriptures among the early believers." That's true, but just look at what was happening with them every day. They were living in revival on a recurring basis. Here are some key scriptures to give you an idea of the Lord's heart and desire to revive us. Hone in on these truths and hear and feel His heart, not just the words:

> *Repent therefore and be converted, that your sins may be blotted out, so that times of refreshing may come from the presence of the Lord, and that He may send Jesus Christ, whom heaven must receive until the times of restoration of all things, which God has spoken by the mouth of all His holy prophets since the world began.*
>
> Acts 3:19-21

> *Will You not revive us again,*
> *That Your people may rejoice in You?*
> *Show us Your mercy, Lord,*
> *And grant us Your salvation.*
>
> *I will hear what God the Lord will speak,*
> *For He will speak peace*

Refresh, Revive, and Restore

To His people and to His saints;
But let them not turn back to folly.

Psalm 85:6-8

Restore us, O God of our salvation,
And cause Your anger toward us to cease.

Psalm 85:4

Repent, then, and turn to God, so that your sins
may be wiped out, that times of refreshing may
come from the Lord, and that he may send the
Messiah, who has been appointed for you—even
Jesus. Acts 3:19-20, NIV

What does it all mean? You and I must turn from our sin, from our own ways, turning to God (that's what repent means) and then the times of refreshing will come from the presence of the Lord Jesus Christ, our Messiah, the King of Glory, the King of Kings, the Lord of Lords, our Savior, our Deliverer, our Healer, our Provider. He will show up at the appointed time, the fullness of time, the perfect moment in time, in His power, His presence, and His glory.

Concerning revival, Pastor John Kilpatrick once said, "God never puts revival on sale. He never discounts it. It always costs the same for every generation." Yes, there is a price for revival, but it's well worth it. The time I spent with him during the now-famous Pensacola Revival was one of the greatest seasons of my life. It was a time for making memories, and experiencing miracles and very special moments in the glory.

Repentance and the preaching and teaching of holiness are hallmarks of true revival. If there is a shallow repentance, there will be a shallow revival, if there is a deep repentance, there will be deep revival, and if there is no repentance, there will be no revival—none.

There are a few things that I am sure of in my heart about revival. Whether it was the Tabernacle in the Wilderness, God's favorite house, or the Temple in Jerusalem, God always had a pattern. Tabernacle worship and Temple sacrifice are patterns for revival.

Revival is a personal thing, and you will know you are revived when the driest parts of your limbs begin to bloom, blossom, and bear fruit, fruit that lasts. The fruit of your repentance will be made manifest for all the world to see and recognize.

The phases and waves of revival will include the refreshing of the Church, the revival of the

Church, and the restoration of the Church. This will come with the purpose of bringing awakening to the world and the transformation of our society. Why? Because in the end, the kingdoms of this world will become the kingdoms of our God and His Christ forever and ever!

This will involve planning and work and someone who is willing to pay the price of dying to self and personal desires, so that others can find life. The seed must fall into the ground and die in order to bring forth abundant life.

Rick Joyner, in his foreword for Dutch Sheets' book, *The River of God*,[1] had much to say about the planning process and the sovereignty of God in revival. I was blessed to be involved in the Brownsville Revival for more than three and a half years and am still in relationship with some of the key players in that incredible move of the Spirit. This includes people like Lila Terhune, head of intercession, Paul Wetzel, my pastor, and John Kilpatrick himself. I had lunch with John just a few weeks ago, and he is planning and pressing in to a new move of the Spirit.

Brownsville was indeed a suddenly, but it required a lot of planning, a lot of prayer, and

1. (Raleigh, NC, Regal House Publishing:1998)

a lot of sacrifice and hard work leading up to that suddenly that took place on Father's Day Morning in 1995. Then, it took great effort, energy, and commitment to host the nations. Many people prayed long and hard for revival, but then, when revival actually hit, half of them hit the floor, and the other half hit the door. The revival just didn't look like what they thought it should, and for many, the price tag was too high.

Jesus dropped a truth bomb on us about counting the cost:

> *For which of you, intending to build a tower, does not sit down first and count the cost, whether he has enough to finish it—lest, after he has laid the foundation, and is not able to finish, all who see it begin to mock him, saying, "This man began to build and was not able to finish"?* Luke 14:28-30

This word came right after He said that our generation refuses to receive the truth because it's His truth. His truth is somehow not our truth. We, of course, have a much better truth than Jesus taught. or, so we think.

Was what Jesus said only for that particular time, a time when there was no television, no internet, and no Facebook. Here's what Jesus said it would cost to be a true disciple of His:

> *Now great multitudes went with Him. And He turned and said to them, "If anyone comes to Me and does not hate his father and mother, wife and children, brothers and sisters, yes, and his own life also, he cannot be My disciple. And whoever does not bear his cross and come after Me cannot be My disciple."*
>
> Luke 14:25-28

True disciples, like true prophets and true teachers, don't ignore and leave out entire sections of Jesus' teachings because they don't meet the modern norm for Christianity and church or don't build a following or fellowship. Who are the true disciples? They are those who want to be *"disciples indeed"*:

> *Then Jesus said to those Jews who believed Him, "If you abide in My word, you are My disciples indeed. And you shall know the truth, and the truth shall make you free."*   John 8:31-32

Here is another truth about being a real disciple. If you abide by Jesus' teachings and try to live them out, it will radically change your attitude and your personality and thus your life. We recite the Scriptures, quote them when we find it convenient, and use them against each other, but if we would be honest with ourselves, we all have a problem walking them out in our daily life.

Jesus said:

> *"A new commandment I give to you, that you love one another; as I have loved you, that you also love one another. By this all will know that you are My disciples, if you have love for one another."* John 13:34-35

Here's another thing Jesus said about love:

> *"If you love Me, keep My commandments. And I will pray the Father, and He will give you another Helper, that He may abide with you forever — the Spirit of truth, whom the world cannot receive, because it neither sees Him nor knows Him; but you know Him, for He dwells with you and will be in you. I will not leave you orphans; I will come to you."* John 14:15-18

Refresh, Revive, and Restore

I don't know about you, but I'm hungry and thirsty for more of God, and hungry hearts everywhere are starting to cry out in unity, with one heart and one mind, from every tribe, tongue, and nation: "Come, Lord Jesus! Come quickly!"

I was birthed in His presence, and I am re-birthed in the fires of revival. We need it today as never before, and the only true revival is revival glory, the manifestation of His presence.

As was foretold, God is turning the hearts of the fathers to the sons and the hearts of the sons to the fathers:

> *For, behold, the day cometh, that shall burn as an oven; and all the proud, yea, and all that do wickedly, shall be stubble: and the day that cometh shall burn them up, saith the LORD of hosts, that it shall leave them neither root nor branch. But unto you that fear my name shall the Sun of righteousness arise with healing in his wings; and ye shall go forth, and grow up as calves of the stall. And ye shall tread down the wicked; for they shall be ashes under the soles of your feet in the day that I shall do this, saith the LORD of hosts.* Malachi 4:1-3, KJV

The Lord of Hosts is the Lord who leads us into battle, He who has fire in His eyes and a scepter in His hand. He says:

> *Behold, I will send you Elijah the prophet before the coming of the great and dreadful day of the* LORD: *and he shall turn the heart of the fathers to the children, and the heart of the children to their fathers, lest I come and smite the earth with a curse.* Malachi 4:5-6, KJV

Let us awaken to this moment in time. Let us not grow weary in our pursuit or in well doing, but let us, you and I, press into the greater glory that is to come. The glory of the latter house shall be greater than the former house (see Haggai 2:9). The shaking continues, even in this moment, and Hebrews 12:27 shows us that anything that can be shaken will be shaken, so that whatever is of the Kingdom may remain.

We are stepping into Kingdom reality, a fresh new dimension and fresh revelation of what Kingdom means. We need healing; we need hope; we need freedom; we need Jesus to show up. This season is the prelude to what is to come. This moment is what Jesus called *"the beginning of sorrows"*:

> *And Jesus answered and said unto them, Take heed that no man deceive you. For many shall come in my name, saying, I am Christ; and shall deceive many. And ye shall hear of wars and rumours of wars: see that ye be not troubled: for all these things must come to pass, but the end is not yet. For nation shall rise against nation, and kingdom against kingdom: and there shall be famines, and pestilences, and earthquakes, in divers places. All these are the beginning of sorrows.*
>
> *Then shall they deliver you up to be afflicted, and shall kill you: and ye shall be hated of all nations for my name's sake. And then shall many be offended, and shall betray one another, and shall hate one another. And many false prophets shall rise, and shall deceive many. And because iniquity shall abound, the love of many shall wax cold. But he that shall endure unto the end, the same shall be saved. And this gospel of the kingdom shall be preached in all the world for a witness unto all nations; and then shall the end come.* Matthew 24:4-14, KJV

There is an Elijah cry going forth from the heart of God: Repent ye! There is resurrection power being released in this hour, like the cry of Christ for His friend, Lazarus. He is even now crying out for His remnant, His Bride, His army, a cry of life:

COME FORTH!
AWAKEN, OH SLEEPER!
ARISE AND SHINE!
ROLL BACK THE STONE!
COME FORTH!

Why? Because it's harvest time. We must pray for the laborers, calling them forth. It's time for the prophetic voices in this generation to make bold declarations and proclamations.

"Allow Me," says the Lord, "to gird you in this hour and lead you where you have never been before, into the new and uncharted waters of the Spirit. As a fresh new wind of my Spirit blows, those who are led by My Spirit will move in freedom, unity, and harmony, and in oneness with Me, My purpose, and My will.

Refresh, Revive, and Restore

"I," says the Lord, "will make a way for those who have ears to hear and eyes to see what the Spirit is saying to His Bride, His Army, His Church. Know that I will unveil, reveal, and heal in a moment of acceleration like a nation being formed in a day. Many will turn and return—the prodigals, the wanders, the wayward, the lost, the broken, the wounded. Consider not the worldly wisdom of this moment, but harken unto My voice, you who are My sheep, and I will lead you through the valley of death. I will anoint you with oil. And I," says the Lord, "will set a table before you in the sight of your enemies."

"The cry on My heart for you in this hour is to arise to the moment, as I refresh you, revive you, and restore to you everything that has been stolen. Yes, expect the restoration of all things. Pursue Me now and recover all. This shall be a year of restitution, a year to get back on track, a year of the comeback, a year of retribution, restitution, recompense, and reward, and still the decade of the mouth. Declare this to be an acceptable year *of the Lord.*"

So, come now, let us repent and turn again, for He is the only name and the only way. There is no other name to call on but the name that is above every other name. There is no other way to the Father but through the Son. If you don't know Jesus, but only know about Him, or if you've known Him for thirty or forty years and this day you choose a fresh start, a new moment, a new heart and want to recommit your heart and your life to answer the call to pick up your cross and follow Him, this is the time.

Yes, you, too, can be refreshed, revived, and restored.

Lord, more than anything, we need a move of Your Spirit. I pray today that You would come and visit Your people. Teach us how to entertain Your presence. Come on in, Lord Jesus. Come, O King of Glory. We say, "Come quickly, Lord Jesus!"

Chapter 2

Back in the Day

Thy mercy, O LORD, is in the heavens; and thy faithfulness reacheth unto the clouds.

Psalm 36:5, KJV

In the fall of 2000, I went to Canada as a missionary. I had been twenty-one years in business, but then the Lord touched me and changed my life completely. I was drawn to visit the revival in Pensacola, Florida, and there I received a serious touch from the Lord in the fires that were burning in that place.

I had grown up pretty much on the streets in a town just outside of Philadelphia. It was a rather low-income area, and we had a blended family long before blended families were looked at and accepted as normal.

Refresh, Revive, and Restore

My dad was a truck driver, a gambler, and a fighter. I left home at eighteen, feeling that I simply had to get away, and I soon got married, but life was hard. I moved from one dead-end job to another, working in a steel plant, on a construction crew, serving as a milkman, and selling insurance. I was living a lifestyle of sin and addiction, and this continued … until I was eventually at the end of myself and in need of change. When I was in a very dark and dry place, the Lord found me and gave me my portion and inheritance:

> *For the LORD's portion is his people;*
> *Jacob is the lot of his inheritance.*
> *He found him in a desert land,*
> *And in the waste howling wilderness;*
> *He led him about, he instructed him,*
> *He kept him as the apple of his eye.*
> *As an eagle stirreth up her nest,*
> *Fluttereth over her young,*
> *Spreadeth abroad her wings, taketh them,*
> *Beareth them on her wings:*
> *So the LORD alone did lead him,*
> *And there was no strange god with him.*
>   Deuteronomy 32:9-12, KJV

In that dry, dark, and desperate place, Jesus stepped down into my life, my heart, and my home. He saved me, baptized me in the Holy Spirit, and delivered me from those life-altering sins, addictions, and other issues. He gave me dreams and visions and led me into business by His Spirit. I had about US $300 to my name at the time, but I gathered four friends in the basement of my house and started a business. I was twenty-seven years old and had two young children, a mortgage payment, and other financial obligations, and no savings to speak of. But a new life in Christ had begun.

I was a brand-new creation, born again in the Spirit, and I decided to follow the Spirit and step out in faith on His Word and start a business I knew almost nothing about. I quit the best job I had ever had up until that point and went on the flying trapeze with no net.

After an amazing God-given career of twenty-one years in the security business, I now had more than a hundred and fifty employees and five different companies in security-related fields. However, I had gone through some difficult life situations, including divorce. I was still a confessing Christian, but my life was once again back in a place of compromise and sin.

For all intents and purposes, I was backslidden and had lost my first love and my zeal for Jesus. I was just going through the motions. I had started to smoke and gamble and compromise in every area of life, but I still went to church and confessed the Lord. Now, He took me and shook me and shocked me by calling me into His service.

"What?" I said, "not me! I have nothing to offer. I'm just an alarm man, a salesman." But I couldn't seem to shake that call. Eventually, I said, "Lord, if You send me, I will go … but only if You go with me." In response, He gave me Exodus 33.

> *And the LORD said unto Moses, Depart, and go up hence, thou and the people which thou hast brought up out of the land of Egypt, unto the land which I sware unto Abraham, to Isaac, and to Jacob, saying, Unto thy seed will I give it: and I will send an angel before thee; and I will drive out the Canaanite, the Amorite, and the Hittite, and the Perizzite, the Hivite, and the Jebusite: unto a land flowing with milk and honey: for I*

will not go up in the midst of thee; for thou art
a stiffnecked people: lest I consume thee in the
way.   Exodus 33:1-3, KJV

The Lord also visited me face to face and assured me that He would go with me.

I was still insecure. I said, "Lord, I am no priest." He then brought me to Psalm 110:4:

The LORD hath sworn, and will not repent,
Thou art a priest for ever after the order of
Melchizedek. (KJV)

Miracles still do happen. God takes the foolish things of this world, the broken vessels, and He works with them and through them for His divine purpose. God shook me to my core, called me by name, and spoke to me in dreams and visions, as in Ezekiel chapters 2 and 3.

He then sent me by dreams, visions, and prophetic confirmation to Pensacola, Florida, to the Brownsville Revival, and then to Bible school. I was forty-nine, and God was turning my life upside down.

He next sent me by dreams, visions, and confirmations to Ashland, Virginia, to Calvary

Pentecostal Campground and Tabernacle to sit under the ministry of Ruth Ward Heflin for the last year of her life. I also met and worked with Joan Gieson, who had served eight years with Kathryn Kuhlman and more than twenty years with the Benny Hinn ministry. I ministered on the prayer team in the wheelchair section with Joan and on the altar testimony team under her leadership at eighteen Benny Hinn crusades and partner conferences.

I was also involved with a wonderful lady, Joyce Stolfus from California, who oversaw the altar testimony team. She served in more than a hundred crusades.

Then, the same God who had saved me and filled me, sending me to the Brownsville Revival, to Calvary Camp, and to the Benny Hinn crusades, sent me to Canada. Again, it was through dreams and visions and a prophetic word. It was the year 2000, and I was fifty-one.

I had shared a word with John and Victoria Irving, who were serving as associate pastors in a church in Canada. I had never met them before prophesying over them in Ashland, Virginia in a Ponderosa Restaurant. I ended up going to do services for three days at the church where they served. There God struck a match, and I ended up staying and ministering every day for seven and a half weeks.

After those meetings, I went to another church, this one in Brantford, Ontario, and ministered there for thirteen weeks; then to Aurora, where we birthed our first church plant, the Gathering Place of Aurora. From there, I went from church to church for twelve or thirteen extended revival meetings.

Along the way, I met and married the love of my life, Mave Moyer. We have walked, worked, and pioneered together what now is known as Eagle Worldwide Ministries, a huge network of churches, ministers, and ministries, with our main offices now at the Hub building in Hamilton, Ontario.

God was always talking to us about birthing and pioneering. He sent John Kelly and C. Peter Wagner into our lives, and then commissioned me as an apostle in 2004. At that moment, something new happened. Stepping out in faith with the Lord brought about the opportunity to plant eight new churches, a Bible school, a campground, and an outreach center that feeds hundreds of people each week for the glory of God—the Kingsway Centre in Hamilton, Ontario. We also birthed an apostolic network of more than two hundred and fifty ministers and have led mission teams to about twenty-five nations.

Needless to say, I encountered some obstacles and hindrances along the way and picked up some hurt, pain, rejection, and other baggage in the process … but God!

In September of 2014, after our summer camp meetings, I was not feeling well. I was in a lot of pain and physical distress, so much so that I didn't go to Israel that fall. Mave went and led the tour without me.

I had just turned sixty-five, but I began having some serious pain and other negative symptoms in my body. I had always been athletic, and my body had never let me down. I hadn't been to a serious doctor's visit in many years. When Mave returned, she was so concerned with the weight loss that we immediately made an appointment with our family doctor. After a personal check-up and blood testing, we waited for some answers.

A friend of mine, who was getting married in October, asked me to be his best man. Making it through the rehearsal was a walk of faith, but I overcame and was there to stand by his side while he made his vows the next day. I'm not sure how I survived that day to the end of dinner, but by the grace of God I made it. The car ride home was quite a nightmare, with every part of my body in pain and extreme discomfort.

After the wedding, I went on a mission trip to Guatemala with Apostle John Kelly, the leader of the International Coalition of Apostolic Leaders. This was a very challenging time. The machinery of my body seemed to be breaking down, and my Job's journey had begun.

When I arrived back home, the pain proceeded to get worse, so much so that Mave took me to the hospital. Our family doctor had set an appointment with Dr. Fraser, an oncologist from the Juravinski Cancer Centre in Hamilton, and when we arrived at the hospital, the information they had on their computer alerted them to the issues I was suffering from.

They immediately helped to relieve the pain. Dr. Fraser diagnosed me with stage-four lymphoma. He said I should get my house in order, but he also said, "We are in it … to WIN it."

With this news, Mave turned as white as a sheet. She had lost her father to lymphoma when she was just a small child. He was in his early thirties. She also lost her brother to the same cancer when he was the same age. We had both known that something was wrong and even serious, but when the doctor delivered his diagnosis, we were shocked and traumatized. How could this be?

Dr. Fraser grabbed a stool and sat down between us. He took our hands and said, "We are going to do whatever we need to do to treat this" and "We are in it to WIN it." We grabbed hold of those words as words of faith from the Lord and used them to make war against the enemy.

My first in-home treatment to get me ready for the R Chop, a specifically formulated chemo for lymphoma, was on Christmas Eve. We didn't even tell our kids, as we were trusting God and didn't feel we needed to put a damper on the blessing of being together for the holidays. For the next nine months, we went every other day for harsh chemotherapy and radiation treatments. There were many side effects that lasted for almost a year.

Because of the pain, I was on eight doses of morphine a day. Every lymph node in my body was infected and inflamed. I couldn't even sleep in my bed because the pain was so bad. Mave bought me a nice Lazy Boy chair that I could sleep in, and she camped out in the living room on the couch every night with me. I lost all the hair on my head and body and thirty-eight more pounds of body weight, but my will to live was strong. We fought the good fight together.

Through it all, we clung to our God-given dreams and the prophetic words we had received that were not yet fulfilled. We helped each other to speak words of life, stay in faith, and make war against the enemy.

Except for a few key prayer people around us, we didn't tell anyone else about what we were experiencing. The Lord told Mave, "Loose lips sink ships. Guard your words and guard your faith."

After nine months of intensive treatment, I was in remission, but I was also very weak and could barely open a door. I needed help with everything and even needed a wheelchair at the airport, but by God's grace, we kept going.

Most of the people around us knew I was going through some sort of a healing challenge, but now we were able to share our testimony and give God the glory for our victory. During that period, a couple of people we knew died from the same type of cancer, but we continued to press into God in faith, trusting that He was not finished with me yet. And, thankfully, He definitely was not!

The Lord showed me He wanted us to move to Pensacola and plant a church there. He said He was taking us "back to the future." We went to do a few services and stir up the fires of revival, but then God told us to stay. A small group of people had been gathering in a rented place. They called it The Dwelling Place. They had already set up a non-profit corporation in the United States. They shared with us that the Lord was speaking to them about us being their apostolic covering and pastors.

Mave and I had pastored every church we ever pioneered, but I had never really considered myself a pastor. People seemed to call me every name in the book, but not usually Pastor. If they did call me Pastor, I would correct them and say, "Brother works just fine." I just didn't think of myself as a pastor.

I was in rough shape physically, but the Lord was refreshing and restoring me, speaking and confirming His Word over me.

REFRESHING, RESTARTING, AND RESETTING—BACK TO THE FUTURE!

Mave was reluctant to move and leave Canada and her family, so I didn't say much to her about it. I didn't want to press the issue because we had been through so much together already. She had been through every appointment and treatment with me and was my primary caregiver through it all.

Ashley Almas, our spiritual daughter and my Elisha in the prophetic mentoring, was also right there in the process, as was my armor bearer, Reid Grassick. They made it as easy as possible for me to meet my commitments, schedule, and travel. Patty Wallace, who had also lived with us as a spiritual daughter for many years, stepped up as the Vice President of operations, and she and Mave handled many of the day-to-day functions during my treatment and recovery.

This crisis was difficult and had taken a toll on all of us, but I am forever grateful to them and to the Lord for their help, faithfulness, and involvement throughout the ordeal.

After a couple of monthly revival meetings, the Dwelling Place group in Florida approached us about being their apostolic overseers and pastors. The Lord had already spoken to Mave and me, and this confirmed it, so we agreed to stay and pastor the Dwelling Place. I was really feeling good.

Two years later, however, while living and leading in Pensacola, I suffered a relapse of the lymphoma. One of my eyes started to dry up and was bothering me. The eye doctor said it was just droopy eye and was "part of getting old," but when I returned to Canada and went to my oncologist for my regular follow-up, he said he was pretty sure it was lymphoma again. The inflamed lymphoid was behind my eye this time and could be very dangerous.

Dr. Fraser sent me to a surgeon who had to do an exploratory operation through the center of my eye. His conclusion was that the cancer was not touching the brain, so they would be able to treat it. Thank God! However, the procedure left me with double vision. The surgeon told me that the double vision would very likely persist but might be corrected with special lenses.

Now we needed to brace ourselves to undergo another regime of steroids, chemotherapy, and radiation. All the while we continued to go back and forth between Canada and the US.

After several weeks of treatment, I went for a check-up with Dr. Fraser, and he talked to Mave and me about the need for me to undergo a stem-cell transplant. It was quite a faith-building and faith-challenging process the next few months as they prepared me for this procedure.

When I was admitted to the hospital for the transplant, they administered a drug to pump up my blood cells. They told us they would need to harvest at least four million cells. If they could not get that many, I would need to have a donor. Since the doctor had told us my own cells were best, we prayed that we would not need a donor. They took the blood through a port in my chest and put it into a machine that cleaned it and removed all of the diseased cells. Then the clean blood was cryogenically frozen so that they could return it disease-free into my body on the third day.

Refresh, Revive, and Restore

The second day they bombarded my system with the harshest chemo they could use. This was to kill everything, both good and bad, in order to rid my body of the diseased cells that were left. The problem was that it almost killed me. At this point, my immune system was non-existent, and I was in a room where even the air and atmosphere were controlled.

On the third day, several doctors gathered around my bed to put the clean cells back into my body. I had an incredible opportunity to share with them the Gospel and my experience with God and His constant goodness in my life. The presence of the Lord was sweet and tangible as they pumped life back into my body.

Dr. Fraser told us it was a medical miracle, and we had to agree with him. It was. God can do His supernatural work in every area and aspect of our lives, as we trust Him and follow after peace.

We struggled through the next few months with good and not-so-good days, as they worked on me to rebuild my immune system. The Lord was with us and recovery surely came ... one day at a time. But the double vision continued to plague me.

When I returned to Pensacola, a good friend of mine, Mark, the $50 Eye Guy, made me a special pair of glasses, but when I walked, they made me dizzy, so I couldn't wear them.

One night I was crying out to God in the meeting about my sight and complaining. The next morning, my vision was restored. I could see again, and I passed the Florida eye test to drive with no glasses at all. Glory to God! He had restored my sight!

In 2020, the scourge of COVID started to spread, and the world we lived in changed dramatically. Everything changed overnight. Church services were shut down. Travel was shut down. Health services suffered. Again, I was refreshed and revived by the power and presence of God. The Lord kept me in a safe place in the palm of His hand. He again began to refresh and revive me, and I made it through even the worst of treatments—a stem-cell transplant and the strongest chemo that could be administered without killing me.

During the time I was recovering, I got very stressed out over moving our home in Canada. For me, the process was emotionally overwhelming, and with the stress and my low immune system, I broke out with shingles up my side, around my neck, and into my ear. We called the doctor, he gave me some medications to treat it, and the rash went away, but afterward I lost all hearing in my right ear (my best ear). The doctor said that when this happens, the hearing almost never comes back. He only knew of one ear doctor who had ever had success with this type of hearing loss, but even then the hearing recovery wasn't good. I had to take the chance.

I had been wearing hearing aids since I was in my twenties and was legally deaf. They began to treat me. About twenty-one days went by. We didn't tell anyone, I kept wearing my hearing aid, and Mave kept yelling in my ear. Finally, one day I said, "It may just be my mind playing tricks on me, but I think I hear a faint sound far off." Over the next three days, my hearing in that ear was restored to the level I had enjoyed before the shingles attack. Glory to God! He had restored my hearing back to the pre-shingles level. He is the God of miracles. He heals, He saves, He refreshes, He revives, and He restores! All was well.

Then, suddenly, I began having bad pain in my back. I was having trouble getting in and out of the car and walking or sitting for more than ten to fifteen minutes, and I was waking up every morning in pain. I went to the doctor, and he sent me for X-rays. The X-ray tech read the X-ray and said I seemed to have a small curvature of the spine. A chiropractor friend prescribed an exercise program, but the pain kept getting worse. Finally, my doctor referred me to the Andrews Institute in Gulf Breeze, Florida. It was, he said, one of the best in the country, and it was only twelve miles away.

At the Andrews Institute, they did what they called "hip-replacement surgery," and I was able to recover in a few months with a little home rehab. I'm now playing golf every couple of weeks and am feeling better than I have in many years.

Our Lord saves, He heals, He delivers, and He changes your life. He restored my sight, my hearing, my health, and my strength. Glory to our God! Jesus is alive, and He hears our prayers. According to His Word, as we delight ourselves in Him, He gives us the desires of our hearts. I now play golf regularly and have a very full work, ministry, and life schedule, including traveling to the nations, and have overcome and recovered from everything I was confronted with. God is good all the time, and all the time God is good.

Although all the glory goes to Him, I am very thankful for every one of my doctors, medical professionals, family, friends, and associates who walked with me. I believe that the Lord alone is the Healer, that doctors can diagnose and treat you, but only God can heal you. It is our faith in God and the prayers, love, and care of faithful friends and family that gets us through these difficult life crises. He refreshes, He revives, and He restores. He is Faithful and True.

He is not a respecter of persons. I can relate in my heart to Paul's testimony, as well as his missionary journey, his struggles, but then his wonderful testimony of God's faithfulness. He delivered me from all.

> *But you have carefully followed my doctrine, manner of life, purpose, faith, longsuffering, love, perseverance, persecutions, afflictions, which happened to me at Antioch, at Iconium, at Lystra—what persecutions I endured. And out of them all the Lord delivered me. Yes, and*

all who desire to live godly in Christ Jesus will
suffer persecution.   2 Timothy 3:10-12

Our God heals, saves, and delivers. If you need a miracle healing in your life or have been diagnosed with a terminal illness or disease, press in now. I want to come into agreement with you in prayer, for I know there is power in prayer and even more power when we come into agreement in prayer.

Hear His voice now, reach out to Him, and receive His touch today. Yes, you, too, can be refreshed, revived, and restored.

Heavenly Father, I come to You in the name of Jesus Christ and in the power of the Holy Spirit and agree with my brother and sister for their miracle breakthrough today, for their healing. We stand in faith and expectation, declaring victory in Your name, healing in Your name. I release hope and peace into Your people today and over their lives and families.

In Jesus' mighty name!

Chapter 3

The Power of Pentecost

*And when the day of Pentecost was fully come,
they were all with one accord in one place. And
suddenly there came a sound from heaven as of a
rushing mighty wind, and it filled all the house
where they were sitting. And there appeared
unto them cloven tongues like as of fire, and it
sat upon each of them. And they were all filled
with the Holy Ghost, and began to speak with
other tongues, as the Spirit gave them utter-
ance.*   Acts 2:1-4, KJV

The power of Pentecost includes the promise
and purpose of God's power, and I personally
believe this is the only answer to the situations
we find ourselves faced with today in the post-
pandemic Church, the twenty-first-century

Church, and society at large. We need a fresh Pentecost, fresh fire, fresh power, a fresh anointing of the Holy Spirit. Nothing short of that will do. This fresh anointing will give us a new heart and a fresh start. This fresh Pentecost will give us the power and boldness to prepare the way for the Second Coming of Christ and to fulfill our own mandate and realize our own destiny.

The power of Pentecost is the power to overcome, the power to win, the power to finish and finish well. This ability to finish will not be accomplished by our own might, nor our own power, but only by the power of God's Spirit. It will not be by our own plans, strategies, or methods. We must tap into the life-giving power of the Holy Spirit, with wisdom and understanding in dreams, visions, and revelation from the heavenlies. We here in North America, the Church, need the presence and the power of God like never before.

I honestly believe that many have drawn closer to the Lord during these years of crisis, but it is also evident that many have drifted and fallen away. When the fire falls, the power of prophecy comes upon the people. We in the end-time Church are a prophetic people, a prophetic generation, a prophetic army. It is God's desire that all His people prophesy.

One of the things that has occurred in the past twenty years, as the Lord is trying to restore His Church and its five-fold government, is that there has been a radical attack on the prophetic and apostolic ministries, the foundational ministries Paul spoke of in Ephesians 2. There is now much division within the Body of Christ concerning the gifts of the Spirit and the office gifts Paul established in Ephesians 4:11-12 as our governmental leadership under the power of the Spirit.

Paul prophesied concerning the end-time moments and season we are in now, that many would have a form of godliness but deny the power thereof. He said that we must flee from this form of religion. He also spoke of the apostasy, the great falling away, that we are obviously experiencing throughout our societies:

> *Now the Spirit expressly says that in latter times some will depart from the faith, giving heed to deceiving spirits and doctrines of demons, speaking lies in hypocrisy, having their own conscience seared with a hot iron.*
>
> 1 Timothy 4:1-2

This searing of the conscience is the absence of the fear of the Lord, which has opened the door to sin and compromise. It is time for a fresh Pentecost.

Moses knew and declared to others that it was God's will for all His people to prophesy:

> *So Moses went out and told the people what the Lord had said. He brought together seventy of their elders and had them stand around the tent. Then the Lord came down in the cloud and spoke with him, and he took some of the power of the Spirit that was on him and put it on the seventy elders. When the Spirit rested on them, they prophesied—but did not do so again.*
>
> *However, two men, whose names were Eldad and Medad, had remained in the camp. They were listed among the elders, but did not go out to the tent. Yet the Spirit also rested on them, and they prophesied in the camp. A young man ran and told Moses, "Eldad and Medad are prophesying in the camp."*
>
> *Joshua son of Nun, who had been Moses' aide since youth, spoke up and said, "Moses, my lord, stop them!"*

But Moses replied, "Are you jealous for my sake? I wish that all the LORD's people were prophets and that the LORD would put his Spirit on them!" Numbers 11:24-29, NIV

Joel confirmed this truth:

And afterward,
I will pour out my Spirit on all people.
Your sons and daughters will prophesy, your old men will dream dreams, your young men will see visions.
Even on my servants, both men and women, I will pour out my Spirit in those days.
I will show wonders in the heavens and on the earth, blood and fire and billows of smoke.
The sun will be turned to darkness and the moon to blood before the coming of the great and dreadful day of the LORD.

Joel 2:28-31, NIV

John the Baptist prophesied the same thing and spoke of the Greater One to come, the One who would baptize us in the Holy Spirit and fire—Jesus:

*I indeed baptize you with water unto repentance,
but He who is coming after me is mightier than
I, whose sandals I am not worthy to carry. He
will baptize you with the Holy Spirit and fire.
His winnowing fan is in His hand, and He will
thoroughly clean out His threshing floor, and
gather His wheat into the barn; but He will
burn up the chaff with unquenchable fire.*

Matthew 3:11-13

This baptism of the Holy Spirit was the answer
to Moses' prayer, and the fulfilment of the prophesies of Joel, John the Baptist and Jesus, and it
came on the Day of Pentecost. This baptism is the
key, the baptism of fire and power. For you and
me, the end-time Church, the Remnant, this is
the key to doing the greater works Jesus foretold:

*Most assuredly, I say to you, he who believes
in Me, the works that I do he will do also; and
greater works than these he will do, because I
go to My Father.*   John 14:12

In the last intimate moments Jesus spent with
His disciples, He spoke of this promise. He said
that He would not leave them alone, He would

not leave them orphans, but that He would send the Spirit of Truth, the Comforter, the Advocate, the Counselor, who would know all things and would guide them (and us) into all truth and bring glory to Jesus.

Jesus ... He is the Way, the Truth and the Life. He said:

> *Let not your heart be troubled; you believe in God, believe also in Me. In My Father's house are many mansions; if it were not so, I would have told you. I go to prepare a place for you. And if I go and prepare a place for you, I will come again and receive you to Myself; that where I am, there you may be also. And where I go you know, and the way you know.*
>
> John 14:1-4

These were Christ's words of comfort, His promise of power, His assurance that He would never leave us alone. The disciples received and walked in this promise:

> *And whatever you ask in My name, that I will do, that the Father may be glorified in the Son. If you ask anything in My name, I will do it.*

Refresh, Revive, and Restore

If you love Me, keep My commandments. And I will pray the Father, and He will give you another Helper, that He may abide with you forever — the Spirit of truth, whom the world cannot receive, because it neither sees Him nor knows Him; but you know Him, for He dwells with you and will be in you. I will not leave you orphans; I will come to you.

A little while longer and the world will see Me no more, but you will see Me. Because I live, you will live also. At that day you will know that I am in My Father, and you in Me, and I in you. He who has My commandments and keeps them, it is he who loves Me. And he who loves Me will be loved by My Father, and I will love him and manifest Myself to him.

John 14:13-21

Our God would never send us into battle without equipping us with everything we needed to be victorious. The Holy Spirit and Christ in us, the Hope of Glory, is what we need to overcome. He is all the power you need or will ever need.

When Jesus was about to ascend back to Heaven, He gave a mandate and commission to His successors. His Mandate, the Messiah Mandate, which He had received as had been prophesied in Isaiah 61, He now gave to the Apostles of the Lamb as recorded in Matthew 10. First came the prophesy, then the mandate, then the promise, then the power to fulfill that mandate:

> *Later He appeared to the eleven as they sat at the table; and He rebuked their unbelief and hardness of heart, because they did not believe those who had seen Him after He had risen. And He said to them, "Go into all the world and preach the gospel to every creature. He who believes and is baptized will be saved; but he who does not believe will be condemned. And these signs will follow those who believe: In My name they will cast out demons; they will speak with new tongues; they will take up serpents; and if they drink anything deadly, it will by no means hurt them; they will lay hands on the sick, and they will recover."*
>
> *So then, after the Lord had spoken to them, He was received up into heaven, and sat down at the right hand of God. And they went out and preached everywhere, the Lord working with*

them and confirming the word through the accompanying signs. Amen. Mark 16:14-20

The Spirit of God reveals and confirms Christ, that He is who He says He is. The Holy Spirit will always bear witness to Christ, and any spirit that brings doubt to that fact is a false and demonic spirit. The Spirit of God always bears witness to the Son.

Luke, the beloved physician, wrote:

The former account I made, O Theophilus, of all that Jesus began both to do and teach, until the day in which He was taken up, after He through the Holy Spirit had given commandments to the apostles whom He had chosen, to whom He also presented Himself alive after His suffering by many infallible proofs, being seen by them during forty days and speaking of the things pertaining to the kingdom of God. Acts 1:1-3

Luke went on to describe the promise:

And being assembled together with them, He commanded them not to depart from Jerusalem, but to wait for the Promise of the Father, "which," He said, "you have heard from Me; for John truly baptized with water, but you shall be baptized with the Holy Spirit not many days from now."

Therefore, when they had come together, they asked Him, saying, "Lord, will You at this time restore the kingdom to Israel?" And He said to them, "It is not for you to know times or seasons which the Father has put in His own authority. But you shall receive power when the Holy Spirit has come upon you; and you shall be witnesses to Me in Jerusalem, and in all Judea and Samaria, and to the end of the earth."

Acts 1:4-8

This passage includes one of the primary purposes of the power of the baptism of fire, and that purpose is that we become witnesses for Christ here, there, and everywhere, even to the ends of the earth.

Then, in the fullness of time, on the Day of Pentecost, the power came. Peter declared:

But this is that which was spoken by the prophet Joel. Acts 2:16, KJV

What had happened? As 120 believers gathered together in one accord in faith and waited in obedience for the promise, suddenly it came. It truly appeared to be suddenly, but it had been ordained and spoken of in many ways and forms for hundreds, even thousands of years. Here's what happened:

> *When the Day of Pentecost had fully come, they were all with one accord in one place. And suddenly there came a sound from heaven, as of a rushing mighty wind, and it filled the whole house where they were sitting. Then there appeared to them divided tongues, as of fire, and one sat upon each of them. And they were all filled with the Holy Spirit and began to speak with other tongues, as the Spirit gave them utterance.* Acts 2:1-4

Peter, who not long before had cringed in fear and denied Christ, had been restored to faith by Christ through His mercy and grace, and he now preached the Gospel for the first time under the power and unction of the Holy Spirit:

The Power of Pentecost

But Peter, standing up with the eleven, raised his voice and said to them, "Men of Judea and all who dwell in Jerusalem, let this be known to you, and heed my words. For these are not drunk, as you suppose, since it is only the third hour of the day. But this is what was spoken by the prophet Joel:

'And it shall come to pass in the last days, says God, That I will pour out of My Spirit on all flesh; Your sons and your daughters shall prophesy, Your young men shall see visions, Your old men shall dream dreams. And on My menservants and on My maidservants I will pour out My Spirit in those days; And they shall prophesy. I will show wonders in heaven above And signs in the earth beneath: Blood and fire and vapor of smoke. The sun shall be turned into darkness, And the moon into blood, Before the coming of the great and awesome day of the LORD. And it shall come to pass That whoever calls on the name of the LORD Shall be saved.'

"Men of Israel, hear these words: Jesus of Nazareth, a Man attested by God to you by miracles, wonders, and signs which God did through Him in your midst, as you yourselves also know—Him, being delivered by the determined purpose and foreknowledge of God, you have taken by lawless hands, have crucified, and put to death; whom God raised up, having loosed the pains of death, because it was not possible that He should be held by it."

Acts 2:14-24

What was the purpose of this power? Here are five wonderful reasons to press in and tarry for this blessing:

1. **To receive boldness and confidence to overcome fear:** Shortly before this enduement from Heaven, these disciples were walking in fear of man, fear of death, fear of punishment, and they cringed in fear that caused them to shrink back in the heat of battle. They scattered, each going his own way, and in one way or another, they denied or abandoned Him in the hour of His greatest need. Now they boldly stepped out publicly and began

their journey with the acts of the Holy Spirit in their lives.

2. **To receive revelation, wisdom, and understanding from God:** These disciples now received dreams and visions with revelation and direction straight from God. They were now able to be truly led by the Spirit.

3. **To receive the power to preach and be witnesses:** This enduement of the Spirit was necessary for them and is necessary for us to answer the Great Commission: "Go ye." It was equally necessary to empower them to obey the great command to love one another, not with a natural love, but with the *agape* love of the Spirit. We are empowered to love the unlovable and also to love our enemies. We must reach deep to find such love in the Spirit.

4. **To be able to reach outside of a building.** These disciples burst out of their building, and it is the same today. The mandate and purpose for the Church in this season is to push out of the four walls of our building and be the Church, not merely attend church.

5. **To be able to birth and build the pioneers of this generation:** The power of Pentecost, a fresh dose of the Holy Ghost, is the ability to build the Church and fight the enemy. It is the power to know and discern the stops and goes, as Peter did with Cornelius and as Paul did with the call to Macedonia. It is a boldness to confront demonic spirits, a boldness to approach the Father in prayer and to know Him as an ever-present Friend. It is the assurance that He lives within us. It is Christ, the Hope of Glory, enabling us to do whatever is needed at the moment.

The encounter the disciples had on the Day of Pentecost, in the fullness of time, was not the end. It was the beginning of a walk of faith and a life in the Spirit. Throughout the New Testament, they continued receiving fresh outpourings and encounters of the Spirit at strategic moments (as in Acts 4:31, where they prayed for signs and wonders to be done in the name of Jesus in the midst of persecution):

> *And when they had prayed, the place where they were assembled together was shaken; and they*

were all filled with the Holy Spirit, and they spoke the word of God with boldness.

Acts 4:31

They continued to operate in the miraculous power of the Spirit, as in Acts 5:12-15:

And through the hands of the apostles many signs and wonders were done among the people. And they were all with one accord in Solomon's Porch. Yet none of the rest dared join them, but the people esteemed them highly. And believers were increasingly added to the Lord, multitudes of both men and women, so that they brought the sick out into the streets and laid them on beds and couches, that at least the shadow of Peter passing by might fall on some of them.

Acts 8 records a great move of the Spirit that occurred when Phillip, the evangelist, preached in Samaria, John and Peter joined him, and the people there received the Holy Spirit.

Acts 10 records a great move of the Spirit that took place with Peter at the home of Cornelius, just as it had on the first day:

Refresh, Revive, and Restore

While Peter was still speaking these words, the Holy Spirit fell upon all those who heard the word. And those of the circumcision who believed were astonished, as many as came with Peter, because the gift of the Holy Spirit had been poured out on the Gentiles also. For they heard them speak with tongues and magnify God. Acts 10:44-46

Let us, you and I, press in to the Lord for a fresh outpouring of His Spirit, His love, and His promise—a fresh Pentecost. Press in, press on, step into this now moment promise and blessing that Peter declared on that first glorious day:

But those things which God foretold by the mouth of all His prophets, that the Christ would suffer, He has thus fulfilled. Repent therefore and be converted, that your sins may be blotted out, so that times of refreshing may come from the presence of the Lord, and that He may send Jesus Christ, who was preached to you before, whom heaven must receive until the times of restoration of all things, which God has spoken by the mouth of all His holy prophets since the world began. Acts 3:18-21

That was then, and this is now, but God has not changed. His will for you is the same.

Yes, you, too, can be refreshed, revived, and restored.

Heavenly Father, I come to You in the name of Jesus Christ and in the power of the Holy Spirit. I pray that You would release over us today, as well as the Church of Jesus Christ, a fresh Pentecost. Lord, we need fresh fire. We need pure fire. We need Your fire. Send the fire again. As it was on the Day of Pentecost, as You have in every season of refreshing, send Your fire today. In Jesus' name.

Chapter 4

The Players, Performers, and Partakers of True Revival

Let all things be done decently and in order.
1 Corinthians 14:40

This chapter is more from personal and practical experience than from a theological perspective. It is a view from "the eye of the storm."

Revival glory is the only true revival. What does that mean? It means reigniting a passion for God's presence. You cannot have true revival unless it comes *in* and *with* His glory. After all, revival is a manifestation of God's power and presence, and we cannot have revival without them.

Again, when I speak about experiencing God's presence, I'm not referring to His omnipresence.

Without a doubt, He is everywhere at once. I'm referring to His manifest presence. He chooses *where* and *when* to reveal His presence in power and glory.

When revival comes, it's not just God that shows up in all His glory. The enemy comes too, but he has a very different agenda. As always, he is intent upon distracting, destroying, killing, and deceiving.

Certain people are also drawn to revival. Some are drawn by the Spirit, and others are drawn by the flesh. Our hope is that these get in the Spirit and leave in the Spirit, but there is no guarantee. When you flip on the lights, sometimes bugs show up, but be careful. It is possible to throw the baby out with the bath water. Test the spirits, but don't be too quick to judge. Why? Because when God shows up, it's not usually the way we may have expected.

If you don't understand something that is happening, pray about it. Lean on the Lord and give yourself some time to observe it and meditate on it. Ask yourself some questions: Is this pointing people toward Jesus? Is the name of Jesus being glorified? If so, handle it with extreme care.

Always keep in mind: when Jesus went forth to save, heal, and deliver, many considered Him to be from the devil:

> *Then Jesus went out from there and departed to the region of Tyre and Sidon. And behold, a woman of Canaan came from that region and cried out to Him, saying, "Have mercy on me, O Lord, Son of David! My daughter is severely demon-possessed."*
>
> *But He answered her not a word.*
>
> *And His disciples came and urged Him, saying, "Send her away, for she cries out after us."*
>
> *But He answered and said, "I was not sent except to the lost sheep of the house of Israel."*
>
> *Then she came and worshiped Him, saying, "Lord, help me!"*
>
> *But He answered and said, "It is not good to take the children's bread and throw it to the little dogs."*
>
> *And she said, "Yes, Lord, yet even the little dogs eat the crumbs which fall from their masters' table."*
>
> *Then Jesus answered and said to her, "O woman, great is your faith! Let it be to you as you desire." And her daughter was healed from that very hour.*

Refresh, Revive, and Restore

Jesus departed from there, skirted the Sea of Galilee, and went up on the mountain and sat down there. Then great multitudes came to Him, having with them the lame, blind, mute, maimed, and many others; and they laid them down at Jesus' feet, and He healed them. So the multitude marveled when they saw the mute speaking, the maimed made whole, the lame walking, and the blind seeing; and they glorified the God of Israel. Now Jesus called His disciples to Himself and said, "I have compassion on the multitude, because they have now continued with Me three days and have nothing to eat. And I do not want to send them away hungry, lest they faint on the way."

Then His disciples said to Him, "Where could we get enough bread in the wilderness to fill such a great multitude?"

Jesus said to them, "How many loaves do you have?"

And they said, "Seven, and a few little fish."

So He commanded the multitude to sit down on the ground. And He took the seven loaves and the fish and gave thanks, broke them and gave them to His disciples; and the disciples gave to the multitude. So they all ate and were filled, and they took up seven large baskets full of the fragments that were left. Now those who ate were four thousand men, besides women and children. And He sent away the multitude, got into the boat, and came to the region of Magdala. Matthew 15:21-39

What should we expect to see today? Signs, wonders, and miracles, gifts of the Spirit, salvations, re-dedications, backsliders and prodigals coming home, people being saved, healed, delivered, called, and sent.

Peter preached:

Repent, then, and turn to God, so that your sins may be wiped out, that times of refreshing may come from the Lord, and that he may send the Messiah, who has been appointed for you—even Jesus. Heaven must receive him until the time comes for God to restore everything, as he promised long ago through his holy prophets. Acts 3:19-21, NIV

As waves of refreshing revival sweep over us, we should experience awakening and transformation. Paul wrote:

Refresh, Revive, and Restore

I beseech you therefore, brethren, by the mercies of God, that ye present your bodies a living sacrifice, holy, acceptable unto God, which is your reasonable service. And be not conformed to this world: but be ye transformed by the renewing of your mind, that ye may prove what is that good, and acceptable, and perfect, will of God.
                                                    Romans 12:1-2, KJV

THE PLAYERS—THE WHO'S WHO AND WHAT'S WHAT OF REVIVAL

Who is involved in revival?

1. The Torchbearer (the evangelist, the messenger, someone God chooses)

2. The Host (the pastor, his team, and their facility. He needs to pastor and protect the move and its integrity and also care for those who are coming to drink and catch the fire.)

3. The Keepers of the Flame (the intercessors and worshippers)

4. The Pages and Scribes (They make important

announcements, prepare important publications and other necessary documents, getting the message out by the media of the age.)

In revival, we also have the performers, the pretenders, and the real partakers:

THE PERFORMERS: Performers may just be looking for their fifteen minutes of fame. Is the revival, for them, just a place to attract attention and demonstrate their gift? Are they interested in drawing attention to themselves? Are they trying to use God's move to promote themselves?

THE PRETENDERS: These are sent by the enemy to distract and disrupt. They have no real hunger for God or His will. Discern their presence and marginalize them, without hindering what God is doing at the moment.

THE GENUINE PARTAKERS: The real partakers are not only hungry for God; they humbly pursue Him with passion and in perfect order. Facilitate them.

Refresh, Revive, and Restore

Revival is fun, but it also involves the hard work of ministry. We must prepare for the worst and believe for the best. We must be firm but loving. We must be sure before we move. We must be humble and willing to change course when it is necessary.

Revival is very contagious, very messy, and hard work, but it is also worth every bit of our effort, energy, and risk. I can say it was the most memorable experience of my life.

Without oxen a stable stays clean,
but you need a strong ox for a large harvest.
Proverbs 14:4. NLT

We must commit to a relentless pursuit of God, His light, His power, His presence, and His glory. Let us pray for true revival, a revival of holiness and hope.

Yes, you, too, can be refreshed, revived, and restored.

Heavenly Father, I thank You for Your goodness, Your mercy, and Your grace. I pray for the laborers, the harvesters, the players, the performers, and partakers of

revival. I call them now from the north, the south, the east, and the west. By the power of Your Holy Spirit, send the loyal, faithful, hard-working servants that are required for this fresh new move of Your Spirit, that You will gather them, like a mother hen gathers her chicks, that You would put these lively stones in the right place as You rebuild the walls. May their spirits be quickened and their hearts submitted as You energize them to this work of service.

In Jesus' name.

Chapter 5

What's Love Got To Do With It ?

Whoever does not love does not know God,
because God is love.　　　　1 John 4:8, NIV

Did I say, "What's love got to do with it?"
Everything, of course. God *is* Love, so it's all
about love. One of the main things going on
right now all across the nations of the world is
that the Lord is trying and testing the love walk
of His Bride, His Remnant, His Church—you
and me. Yes, the hearts of men and the hearts
of nations are being weighed, tried, and tested.

We are in a season in which the line is getting wider, clearer, and more deeply defined.
God is separating the sheep from the goats,
preparing us for a great season of harvest. Love
is the ticket, and He is even now announcing,

"All aboard!" This revival train is preparing to depart.

God's desire is for His people to be in unity and harmony, for unity is the prelude to blessing. Psalm 133 speaks beautifully of the commanded blessing of unity and alignment:

> *How good and pleasant it is*
>   *when God's people live together in unity!*
> *It is like precious oil poured on the head,*
>   *running down on the beard,*
> *running down on Aaron's beard,*
>   *down on the collar of his robe.*
> *It is as if the dew of Hermon*
>   *were falling on Mount Zion.*
> *For there the LORD bestows his blessing,*
>   *even life forevermore*   Psalm 133:1-3, NIV

When we see true unity, we can know that we have successfully crossed the man-made barriers of denomination, and also of tribe, tongue, and nation, drawing and gathering the generations together. We must receive this as a sign of the streams coming together and know that it is a prelude to the great end-time move of God's Spirit.

What we are currently seeing unfold before our eyes is a falling away, a regathering of the eagles, an acceleration of time, and a commanded blessing upon unity. Let us, therefore, prepare our hearts for tomorrow, knowing that the fullness of the great harvest is near at hand.

The love I'm speaking of in this chapter is true love, not the Hollywood love or the man-made love that operates according to worldly standards. This is the *agape* love, the love that allows us to flow together from different streams, cultures, and traditions. This love allows us to accept, receive, and honor one another and the gift and call of God we each have. It allows us to see and appreciate the unique plan of God and experience His love through each other, no longer competing with one another, but completing one another, recognizing that we are one body, brothers and sisters, sons and daughters in Christ. And we are better together.

This true love lets us celebrate one another with all our triumphs and victories, knowing that we are one. It leaves no place for envy and jealousy but, rather, paves the way to rejoicing in one another, encouraging one another, and standing with one another. This common ground can only be found in Christ, for at the foot of the cross, we are all equal and all one.

> *Beloved, let us love one another, for love is of God; and everyone who loves is born of God and knows God. He who does not love does not know God, for God is love. In this the love of God was manifested toward us, that God has sent His only begotten Son into the world, that we might live through Him. In this is love, not that we loved God, but that He loved us and sent His Son to be the propitiation for our sins. Beloved, if God so loved us, we also ought to love one another.* 1 John 4:7-11

The Lord's Prayer for us is not the "Our Father" we grew up with. That prayer was a teaching model that Jesus shared with His disciples (and with us). His prayer for us is found in John 17:

> *I do not pray for these alone, but also for those who will believe in Me through their word; that they all may be one, as You, Father, are in Me, and I in You; that they also may be one in Us, that the world may believe that You sent Me.*

And the glory which You gave Me I have given them, that they may be one just as We are one: I in them, and You in Me; that they may be made perfect in one, and that the world may know that You have sent Me, and have loved them as You have loved Me.

Father, I desire that they also whom You gave Me may be with Me where I am, that they may behold My glory which You have given Me; for You loved Me before the foundation of the world. O righteous Father! The world has not known You, but I have known You; and these have known that You sent Me. And I have declared to them Your name, and will declare it, that the love with which You loved Me may be in them, and I in them. John 17:20-26

God loved us so much that He sent His best, His only begotten Son, to die in our place, and He did it while we were still sinners. He truly loved us before we ever loved Him.

This God kind of love is strong and powerful. It confronts evil and sin, prejudice, and injustice. I'm talking about the love that brings correction in grace when necessary and stands for truth in the face of adversity. This love walks in Christ's footsteps, hates what He hates and loves what He loves. This love brings forth honor, respect, and reverence, for God and for our fellow man. Jesus said:

> *If you love Me, keep My commandments.*
>
> John 14:15

> *If you hold to my teaching, you are really my disciples. Then you will know the truth, and the truth will set you free.* John 8:31-32, NIV

> *For God so loved the world that He gave His only begotten Son, that whoever believes in Him should not perish but have everlasting life.*
>
> John 3:16

Jesus demonstrated His and the Father's great love toward us and His love and obedience to the Father in John 15:

> *As the Father has loved me, so have I loved you. Now remain in my love. If you keep my commands, you will remain in my love, just as I have kept my Father's commands and remain in his love. I have told you this so that*

my joy may be in you and that your joy may be complete. My command is this: Love each other as I have loved you. Greater love has no one than this: to lay down one's life for one's friends. You are my friends if you do what I command. John 15:9-14, NIV

What is this God kind of love like? It is unconditional and long-suffering.

There are other distinguishing signs of God's love that reflect His character and nature, such as patience, generosity, humility, courtesy, restraint, joy, and consistency. These demonstrate the fruit of the Spirit spoken of in Galatians 5. The apostle Paul exhorted us that against this kind of love there is no defense:

But the fruit of the Spirit is love, joy, peace, longsuffering, kindness, goodness, faithfulness, gentleness, self-control. Against such there is no law. And those who are Christ's have crucified the flesh with its passions and desires. If we live in the Spirit, let us also walk in the Spirit. Let us not become conceited, provoking one another, envying one another.

Refresh, Revive, and Restore

Galatians 5:22-26

There is no greater description of the unfailing *agape* love of Christ in action than Paul shared in 1 Corinthians 13:

> *Love suffers long and is kind; love does not envy; love does not parade itself, is not puffed up; does not behave rudely, does not seek its own, is not provoked, thinks no evil; does not rejoice in iniquity, but rejoices in the truth; bears all things, believes all things, hopes all things, endures all things.*
>
> *Love never fails. But whether there are prophecies, they will fail; whether there are tongues, they will cease; whether there is knowledge, it will vanish away. For we know in part and we prophesy in part. But when that which is perfect has come, then that which is in part will be done away.* 1 Corinthians 13:4-10

Yes, love has everything to do with it, and we must be deliberate in our mission to manifest this God kind of love to a dark, hurting, and broken world, a world that has been abused and betrayed. Men and women, boys and girls alike all want to know that we care about them.

Many of them have lost their ability to love and trust, and they need us to demonstrate the incredible love Christ has extended to us in a real and tangible manner. It will be that love that turns them to repentance. It will be that love, so unmistakable in us, that draws them to Christ.

In order for us to demonstrate this God kind of love, we must first tap into it and receive it for ourselves. If we attempt to show this kind of love to others without first experiencing it for ourselves, it will be little more than empty words.

You and I must go deeper in our relationship with Christ, we must embrace what He has done for us, recognizing and appreciating the life He lived, the price He paid, and the true difference He has made *for* us and *in* us. If we listen with the ears of our hearts, we can hear in this moment His cry, deep calling unto deep, and we can know Him personally and experience His life-changing love.

Let us, you and I, commit ourselves today to a deeper walk with God. Let us fly closer to the flame ... in prayer, in praise, in worship, in relationship. We cannot achieve our goals with good works alone. It is this amazing love that will make all the difference in the world. Love is what makes the world go round, this love that changed you and me. If we are to be the world changers and history makers God has ordained us to be, then love has everything to do with it.

Here is a simple but sure road to restoration that the apostle Paul spoke about to the Corinthian believers of his day:

> *Finally, brothers and sisters, rejoice! Strive for full restoration, encourage one another, be of one mind, live in peace. And the God of love and peace will be with you.*
>
> 2 Corinthians 13:11, NIV

Yes, you, too, can be refreshed, revived, and restored.

My prayer today is that everyone who looks upon you and me would see the love and the light of the Lord Jesus Christ in us, that His love would shine to us and through us today and every day, and that the world would know us by this love, that we are His and He is ours, and that we are one in Him, the Hope of Glory!

Chapter 6

Revival, a Deeper Prophetic Perspective

In the middle of its street, and on either side of the river, was the tree of life, which bore twelve fruits, each tree yielding its fruit every month. The leaves of the tree were for the healing of the nations. Revelation 22:2

Because I was birthed and re-birthed in the fires, seasons, sights, and sounds of revival, those who are around me for very long know that I will be sharing the memories, moments, and miracles. However, not everyone we meet today is of the same mindset or perspective concerning revival. In fact, talk of revival can often provoke powerful opposition, and you more than likely will get as many negative reactions as positive, even to the validity of the term *revival*. You and I who have experienced the life-giving power of the move of God's Spirit share these experiences in common. Since I am prophetic by root gifting, I always want to view things through God's eyes and His heart. I want to get His perspective.

There are words, terms, signs, and symbols that provoke our immediate thought toward revival. These would include words such as *wind, rain, fire, train,* and *river*. When I receive a dream, vision, or revelation and any of these elements appears, it is normally symbolic of revival.

In my book, *Night Watch: Unlocking Your Destiny through Dreams and Visions,*[1] I explain the interpretation of dreams and have a section on signs and symbols that help us to understand better what the Lord is trying to say to us. In order to turn our revelations into something tangible and practical, we need more than the revelation. We need understanding and wisdom.

When I am training others in their prophetic gift or call and hearing the voice of the Lord, the root scripture I always come back to is Paul's apostolic prayer in Ephesians 1:

1. (Greenwell Springs, LA, McDougal & Associates: 2018)

Therefore I also, after I heard of your faith in the Lord Jesus and your love for all the saints, do not cease to give thanks for you, making mention of you in my prayers: that the God of our Lord Jesus Christ, the Father of glory, may give to you the spirit of wisdom and revelation in the knowledge of Him, the eyes of your understanding being enlightened; that you may know what is the hope of His calling, what are the riches of the glory of His inheritance in the saints, and what is the exceeding greatness of His power toward us who believe, according to the working of His mighty power.

Ephesians 1:15-19

Each of the symbols I mentioned that invoke thoughts of revival give us a little different prophetic perspective on what revival looks like and what we can expect. Let's look at some of them more closely:

THE WIND OF GOD

When I see or hear the wind of the Spirit, I think of the power of God released on the Day of Pentecost or on Father's Day in 1995 at

Brownsville Assembly of God. The latter was to begin one of the greatest and longest-lasting revivals in modern Church history. A mighty rushing wind or the wind of the Spirit stirring in the top of the mulberry trees speaks of God stirring up the gifts of the Spirit in me. A gentle breeze might speak of Him bringing me His peace, love, and healing. These are all related to a move of the Spirit, and I then take that revelation and press into it in faith and expectation.

The wind of God reminds me that, in 1976, God found me in desperation in the midst of my sin and hopelessness, He picked me up and has cared for me, carrying me on His wings of love. His wind reminds me over and over again of His faithfulness. This lets me know that regardless of what I happen to be going through or what the circumstances are like in the world around me, He will show up and win the day for me.

> *He found him in a desert land*
> *And in the wasteland, a howling wilderness;*
> *He encircled him,*
> *He instructed him,*
> *He kept him as the apple of His eye.*

As an eagle stirs up its nest,
Hovers over its young,
Spreading out its wings, taking them up,
Carrying them on its wings,
So the LORD alone led him,
And there was no foreign god with him.
He made him ride in the heights of the earth,
That he might eat the produce of the fields;
He made him draw honey from the rock,
And oil from the flinty rock.

Deuteronomy 32:10-13

Therefore, I lean on the heart of God and pray that what He has spoken will come to pass. I'm sure of this: there is a fresh wind blowing today all over the Earth, something new, wonderful, and special for this moment and this generation. Lord, let the wind of Your Spirit blow on us today!

Revival Fire

The fire of revival is not a candle in the window; it is the purifying Refiner's fire of Malachi chapter 3 that prepares the way for the Day of His coming and refines and purifies our hearts:

Behold, I send My messenger,
And he will prepare the way before Me.
And the Lord, *whom you seek,*
Will suddenly come to His temple,
Even the Messenger of the covenant,
In whom you delight.
Behold, He is coming,"
Says the Lord of hosts.
"But who can endure the day of His coming?
And who can stand when He appears?
For He is like a refiner's fire
And like launderers' soap.
He will sit as a refiner and a purifier of silver;
He will purify the sons of Levi,
And purge them as gold and silver,
That they may offer to the Lord
An offering in righteousness."

Malachi 3:1-3

I am not afraid of God or of His fire because I know that He loves me, and He has proven that love over and over. When He called me out of business and marketplace ministry and directed me to Pensacola, Florida, in 1997, to the fires of revival, I had the honor and privilege of sitting under the ministry of Evangelist Steve Hill,

Pastors John Kilpatrick and Paul Wetzel, and Dr. Michael Brown almost every day and night for more than three years. It was the fire of revival and a deep cry and anointing for repentance and holiness that transformed me into who I am and have become. Don't ever fear God, but do have a healthy trust, faith, and reverence for Him. This is known in the Bible as *"the fear of the Lord."*

When I see, hear, feel, or sense revival fire, I open my heart wide and yield and submit to the Spirit in holy reverence for what He is trying to do in me. With an urgency and desire to experience Him, I know this: there is a fire in the river of God that refines us and brings forth the gold and the silver in us. This fire burns up the chaff and reveals the best in us. Send the fire again, Lord! Send more fire!

THE RAIN

When I think of rain, I think of the showers of refreshing God promised in Acts 3:19-21. This softens my heart to turn again to Him and His ways:

Refresh, Revive, and Restore

Repent therefore and be converted, that your sins may be blotted out, so that times of refreshing may come from the presence of the Lord, and that He may send Jesus Christ, who was preached to you before, whom heaven must receive until the times of restoration of all things, which God has spoken by the mouth of all His holy prophets since the world began.

Acts 3:19-21

Rain also reminds me of the streams in the desert of Isaiah or the flash floods that break through and make a way where there is no way. Oh, Lord, let it rain! Send the rain!

When it rains in Israel, they count it as a blessing from God. Lord, send forth those showers of blessing that bring forth a harvest, the former and the latter rain together:

Behold, I will do a new thing,
Now it shall spring forth;
Shall you not know it?
I will even make a road in the wilderness
And rivers in the desert.   Isaiah 43:19

THE RIVER OF GOD

Rivers bring refreshing and new life. The river of God is described in Revelation 22 as a river of life coming from the throne of God. He is the God of revival, and His river is clean and pure. That river brings life, yields fruit, and brings healing to the nations. His river of revival brings you face to face with Him in the glory of His presence:

> *And he showed me a pure river of water of life, clear as crystal, proceeding from the throne of God and of the Lamb. In the middle of its street, and on either side of the river, was the tree of life, which bore twelve fruits, each tree yielding its fruit every month. The leaves of the tree were for the healing of the nations. And there shall be no more curse, but the throne of God and of the Lamb shall be in it, and His servants shall serve Him. They shall see His face, and His name shall be on their foreheads. There shall be no night there: they need no lamp nor light of the sun, for the Lord God gives them light. And they shall reign forever and ever.*
>
> Revelation 22:1-5

Refresh, Revive, and Restore

The river of God in revival is always fresh and new. Sister Ruth Heflin always said that every time you step into the river of God, you are stepping into a new place in that river. You may step in from the same place on the bank as you did before, but you always step into a new place in the river. Why? Because that river is flowing, changing, and bringing something new every day.

In the summer of 2000, I had a vision of the river during worship at Calvary Campground in Ashland, Virginia. The river was flowing from under a doorway in Heaven and started to flow down the main Street of that town. It went past the courthouse, the school, and the business section, and then it turned left. Suddenly, I saw men fishing from its banks. They were just country boys with a stick and a line. They would bait their hook and throw it in, and immediately catch one fish, then another. They got so excited they started throwing the hook back in without any bait, and still they caught fish without it.

Then, suddenly, the fish started jumping out of the water all by themselves and lined up with the other fish the men had already caught. As I watched this, the Lord said, "As My river begins to flow from the throne, it will affect schools, hospitals, the court system, and the market-place, and it will bring forth a supernatural harvest of transformation to every aspect of society." Let it flow, Lord! Let it flow!

A TRAIN

A train has always spoken of revival. Train tracks speak of a parallel unending work of God.

Back in 2000, when God launched me into Canada, one of the most powerful worship albums at that time was "Revival in Belfast" by Robin Marks. God had sent me with a prophetic anointing and a heart for revival. Two of the songs on that album — "Days of Elijah" and the title song, "Revival" — seemed to follow me as I was going from place to place. We had extended revival meetings, some of them for four weeks, some for eight weeks, some for thirteen weeks, and one for twenty-six weeks of services every night. Sometimes we were conducting meetings simultaneously in two different cities. That train was unstoppable.

Refresh, Revive, and Restore

A train is symbolic of you or the Church being on track to the proper destination, and there is always something new coming down the track.

A wonderful and seasoned prophet and friend, Bobby Connor, visited our church and campground in Hamilton, Ontario a number of times, starting in 2003. He received this teaching as a prophetic word in 1997. Many years later, he declared and delivered it while stomping his foot on our hub church, The Revival Centre at 73 Emerald Street in North Hamilton, Ontario. There were so many parallels that I was compelled to receive his message at my very core. Hamilton is still the city of our apostolic revival hub, and we still have a Kingdom view with a local focus, reaching out to the underprivileged in our community at The Kingsway Outreach Centre.

I had a dramatic prophetic vision experience on January 8, 1997. As the vision started, I saw a very intense white light. The light began to sweep over me, and a voice of someone standing to my right in the light said, "Look what is coming down the track and around the bend. It is God's Gold and Diamond Train." Suddenly, I saw the train tracks. One side of the track was named "Truth," and the other side was named "Spirit."

These tracks were coming around the bend of a mountain pass. I could see a very large cloud of what looked like dust and steam. I heard a loud sound as a huge locomotive came into view. I was facing into a light on the front of the engine that was now so intense that it took a lot of effort just to face it.

As it came closer, there was a great disturbance from the sight and sound of this great locomotive. Through the dust and ashes, I could barely see the name on the front of the engine. Across the top was written the word "Judgment" and on the bottom was written "Mercy." As the train moved, the names would rotate so that at one time Judgment would be on the top and then it would reverse, and Mercy would be on the top.

As the train came closer, I saw that the cars were not filled with gold and diamonds, as I had expected, but with coal. I was disappointed because I had been told that I was going to see "God's Gold and Diamond Train." Then the voice of the one standing near my right side said, "Yes, this is God's Gold Train."

Then I heard the Lord Himself say, "This is My Goal Train." I then knew He was speaking of equipping and training. He then said, "There will be plenty of true diamonds and real gold after the heat and pressure that are coming." I knew that He was speaking of refining, and the passage in Malachi 3 came to my heart. The King James Version says it like this:

> *Behold, I will send my messenger, and he shall prepare the way before me: and the LORD, whom ye seek, shall suddenly come to his temple, even the messenger of the covenant, whom ye delight in: behold, he shall come, saith the LORD of hosts.*
>
> *But who may abide the day of his coming? And who shall stand when he appeareth? for he is like a refiner's fire, and like fullers' soap:*
>
> *And he shall sit as a refiner and purifier of silver: and he shall purify the sons of Levi, and purge them as gold and silver, that they may offer unto the LORD an offering in righteousness.*
>
> Malachi 3:1-3, KJV

I was then told that the coming volcanic activity near Bend, Oregon, would announce the beginning of one of the greatest healing revivals in history. This healing revival would start around Hamilton and then blaze across Canada to Vancouver. From there, it would turn down the Northwest Coast of the U.S. and cross the Pacific to the Far East.

I was then told to spell locomotive "local-motive." The Lord said that this local area in the Northwest was a seedbed of the healing anointing that had been upon John G. Lake. The sign of volcanic activity around Bend, Oregon meant that the Lord was turning up the heat, but it would bring about a refining and purifying of His people so that He could release healing in the Earth in an unprecedented way.

The voice which was speaking then said to me, "Have you ever seen anything like this?" I looked and saw the very top of a mountain covered with pure white snow. I was carried to the rim so that I could look over into the large open top of the mountain. It was filled with beautiful, clear, boiling water. I knew that this was the Word of God.

The last thing I saw was a light shining on a diamond, which brought out the brilliant colors that were within the beautiful gem.

Each of these revelations prompts me to pray, to press in, to believe, and to intercede for revival, a sovereign move of God that would sweep across the nations. Worldwide revival ... that's my heart cry. Revive us again, oh God! Let Your fire fall! Let Your wind blow! Let Your glory come down!

As God reveals to you these or other symbols of revival, believe, press in, and be determined to receive. Yes, you, too, can be refreshed, revived, and restored.

Heavenly Father, I thank You that there is a fresh wind blowing, that You are going to bring the latter and the former rain together. Let Your fire fall. Let Your river flow. Let rivers of living water flow through us. Father, I ask You for healthy boundaries, for covenant relationships, for each of us, that You would plant us on the banks of the river of revival and that we would bear fruit in every season, that we would catch every wave and bear fruit that lasts, that not one would miss their moment, that all would get on board, that not one seed would fall to the ground, that the fullness of the harvest that You ordained for each of us would come to fruition.

In Jesus' name.

Chapter 7

Okay, Big Shot, What Are You Going to Do About It?

What will you do in the appointed day,
And in the day of the feast of the LORD?

Hosea 9:5

This is exactly what God said to me on a number of occasions after He had given me a directive or assignment. Many times, this was after we had been back and forth, wrestling with all the possibilities, potentials, and also possible pitfalls, and after I had aired my inabilities, insecurities, hopes, dreams, and fears. He waited on me, He contended with me, and He said everything that needed saying. Then, there was silence, and then the biggie, "What are you going to do now, Big Shot?"

Refresh, Revive, and Restore

I'm definitely a hard-headed kid from just outside of Philly. Half Italian and half Dutch, from a blended family before blended families were in style. You want to know which half was the Italian half? It's the half I have to take to the cross first thing in the morning every day or it will eat my lunch.

My pastor, Paul Wetzel, told me more than once: "A big shot is nothing more than a little shot away from home." Like every man and woman I know who is honest with him- or herself, I have had my battles with pride and sexual sin. These are battles every man and woman face.

I'm not tall, dark, and handsome with black wavy hair; I'm not a great speaker; and I'm not unusually intelligent, like a rocket scientist or a brain surgeon. At the same time, this is also not my first rodeo. My grandparents came over on the boat, but not yesterday. I've been around awhile ... if you know what I mean. I'm really not complicated and do my best to keep things simple and practical.

When I was a young man, like the apostle Peter, I girded myself and went about doing what I wanted and thought was best. Then, when I grew up and came to Christ at twenty-seven, everything changed. He turned me and my little piece of the world totally upside down. I became a man. Then the Holy Spirit girded me and led me into a life and into a place I didn't understand and didn't really want.

When I was young in the Lord, I was much like the apostle Paul, mocking the church and Christian people. I said to the Lord, "If I ran my business the way they run Your Church, I'd be out of business." Yet, as I continued to grow in God and began to take positions of leadership in the Church, I realized that leading the Church was a hundred times more difficult than leading in business. Now, it wasn't just about dollars and cents; now the hearts and souls of God's people were at stake.

This new leadership wasn't a game like the sports I had played and coached over the years. It was about life and death—mine and others. Leading the Church carried with it the greatest sense of responsibility I'd ever known. In many cases, it was the exact opposite of the world I'd lived in.

I found that the Kingdom of God was an upside-down kingdom. If you wanted to be great, you had to be the least and a servant to all. In the world, the leader was always on the top, but in the Kingdom, God's people were on top, and the leader was to be a servant to all of them, as well as to the King.

The worldview was that the one who died with the most toys wins. In the world, toys and money are badges, trophies, and symbols of success. In the Kingdom, these same things can become obstacles and idols. They were really meant to be tools and weapons, and we must know how to handle them, or they will overpower us.

When I graduated from Bible school at forty-nine years old, the Lord asked me if I wanted a good position with salary and benefits or if was I willing to live by faith. I answered quickly, "I trust You. I have lived by faith in business for more than twenty years."

And He said, "Good, it works better by faith."

I said, "I feel called to itinerate ministry, not to pastoral work."

He said, "Do you want the big churches or the small churches?"

I said, "I like the small churches and small places."

He said, "Good, because I was born in the manger, not the palace." Then He spoke this scripture to me:

Do not fear, little flock, for it is your Father's good pleasure to give you the kingdom.

Luke 12:32

This whole issue of life and ministry in Christ is not about fortune and fame; it's about relationship and love. It's not about an income; it's about the outcome. The Kingdom of God is not built of bricks and mortar but of hearts and souls. When we build the Kingdom, we must remember that Jesus said that the Kingdom is within. When we build into people, we are building the Kingdom. When we build value, love, and relationship into people, we are building the Kingdom. It's all about the King and His Kingdom, His people.

When we think, for even a moment, that we can handle things, we will begin to hold on to things, and they will have a hold on us. Deception and pride are already at work. We are only passing through this life, and we don't really own anything for eternity. We are only responsible for stewarding what belongs to God.

In the Kingdom, it's not about what you *would like* to do, and it's not about what you think you *should* do. It's about what you actually do. Good intentions and good ideas are wonderful, and words are powerful, but what it really comes down to is this: what will you actually do with what God has spoken to you? That's what obedience is all about.

I often say that I live by dreams, visions, and prophetic revelation and confirmation. However, I don't just want to be known as a dreamer of dreams. Almost all men and women dream big dreams, but then there are a few men and women who wake up, put their boots on the ground and put their hand to the plow, and start making their dreams become a reality. These are the visionaries, the pioneers. They are the risk-takers who decide not to be mere spectators in life, but are willing to get in the ring and live out their dreams.

Theodore Roosevelt stated it well in his oft-quoted speech "Citizenship in a Republic" given in Paris, France, on April 23, 1910 after he was out of office. One notable passage from the speech is referred to as "The Man in the Arena":

> It is not the critic who counts; not the man who points out how the strong man stumbles, or where the doer of deeds could

have done them better. The credit belongs to the man who is actually in the arena, whose face is marred by dust and sweat and blood; who strives valiantly; who errs, who comes short again and again, because there is no effort without error and shortcoming; but who does actually strive to do the deeds; who knows great enthusiasms, the great devotions; who spends himself in a worthy cause; who at the best knows in the end the triumph of high achievement, and who at the worst, if he fails, at least fails while daring greatly, so that his place shall never be with those cold and timid souls who neither know victory nor defeat. Shame on the man of cultivated taste who lets refinement to develop in to fastidiousness that unfits him for doing the rough work of a work day world.[1]

What should we do? First and foremost, seek God for what He is doing and what He wants you to do. Just as the prophet Habakkuk instructed us in the book that bears his name:

---

1. https://en.wikipedia.org/wiki/Citizenship_in_a_Republic

Refresh, Revive, and Restore

I will stand my watch and set myself on the
rampart,
And watch to see what He will say to me,
And what I will answer when I am corrected.
Then the LORD answered me and said:

"Write the vision
And make it plain on tablets,
That he may run who reads it.
For the vision is yet for an appointed time;
But at the end it will speak, and it will not lie.
Though it tarries, wait for it;
Because it will surely come,
It will not tarry.
Behold the proud,
His soul is not upright in him;
But the just shall live by his faith."

Habakkuk 2:1-4

1. **Go to God.** Seek Him in your special place, your secret place. Seek Him with all your heart, with all you are, all you have, and all you hope to be in Him. Purpose in your heart to align yourself with His will, His purpose, and with His Kingdom vision.

2. **Get in your place in the Body of Christ.** Get in a local church and into proper spiritual alignment, where you can understand the vision and come into agreement with that vision. Develop the godly relations He has ordained for you in this safe place, a place where you can be discipled and mentored, equipped, and prepared.

3. **Once you get the revelation, then continue to seek God for understanding, wisdom, clarity, and timing.** Don't be in a hurry. Wait on God. Get prepared, trained, equipped, and empowered. The process is different with each one of us, but it does take time, and it's too important to skip over. We need to go from revelation to vision, vision to mission, mission to strategy, and strategy to action. The vision must resonate in your spirit as being from God, and, if it is, it will energize you, excite you, and attract everything you need for its fulfilment.

4. **Sit down in the quiet of your room, in the quiet of your heart, and write down the**

vision. Now, turn the vision into an action plan that you can see and believe in your heart, and then implement in a practical, effective, and systematic way.

5. **Seek God-ordained counsel for your life.** There is wisdom in numbers and in the counsel of many, not worldly counsel and not just any counsel, but counsel from those whom God has brought into your life for this specific purpose.

6. **Finally, step up, step in, and step out into everything God has for you.**

My prayer for you today is this:

- **That God would give you revelation, wisdom, and understanding.**
- **That He would refresh you, revive you, and restore you, along with anything and everything that has been stolen from you and your family.**
- **That He would use you as a vessel of reconciliation and restoration in**

> your family, community, church, and
> nation.
>
> - **That everything and everyone you
>   touch will be blessed and brought to
>   new life in Christ.**
> - **That a fresh anointing would come
>   upon you with fresh vision, fresh hope,
>   and fresh fire.**
> - **That the love and the light of the Lord
>   would shine to you and through you,
>   so that everyone who sees you would
>   see Jesus in you.**
> - **That He would bless you and that His
>   great love and favor would rest upon
>   you.**
> - **That you would bear fruit and fruit
>   that lasts.**
>
> **In Jesus' mighty name!**

I believe in the power of prayer and the power
of blessing, and I declare this priestly blessing
over you today and put His name upon you:

> *The LORD bless you and keep you;*
> *The LORD make His face shine upon you,*
> *And be gracious to you;*

Refresh, Revive, and Restore

The LORD lift up His countenance upon you,
And give you peace.   Numbers 6:24-26

Yes, you, too, can be refreshed, revived, and restored.

JOIN US!

EAGLE WORLDWIDE WINTER AND SUMMER CAMP

Eagle Worldwide Ministries provides opportunities each year to fellowship, equip, and empower our Monthly Partners, Network Members, and all those hungry for the presence of the Lord. With guest speakers, nightly services, radical tabernacle worship, prophecy, signs and wonders, the Lord shows up in power in our midst!

Make plans to join Dr. Russ Moyer for one or both of our biannual camp meetings.

Summer Camp
July & August
Hamilton ON || Aurora ON

Winter Camp
January & February
Pensacola, FL

www.eagleworldwide.com // @EagleWorldwideMinistries

PERSONALIZED MENTORING!!

WITH DR. RUSS MOYER

Are you looking to take hold of everything God has for you in this moment and press into the destiny you were created for?

The Screaming Eagles personalized mentoring group is for you! Each group is customized to a particular topic from leadership and the prophetic to spiritual warfare. Dr. Russ takes practical life experiences from over 25 years in ministry and imparts to the next generation.

Email ashley@eagleworldwide.com for more details on how you can become a Screaming Eagle!

SCREAMING EAGLES

EAGLE
WORLDWIDE MINISTRIES
NETWORK

Credentialing
Spiritual Covering
Pastoral Support
Equipping
Networking

Find out how you can become a part of a family of ministers and ministries around the world having Kingdom impact!

As a five-fold ministerial network we value relationship, knowing those that labor among us, giving you the freedom to move and operate in the giftings God has placed in your life.

To find out if our Network is right for you, contact us using the information provided below.

(CAD)
P.O. BOX 39
COPETOWN ON L0R1J0
905.308.9991

(USA)
P.O. BOX 4357
PENSACOLA FL 32507
850.478.0895

www.eagleworldwidenetwork.com

PROPHETS WALKING TOGETHER IN UNITY TO DECLARE THE WORD OF THE LORD.

As the largest coalition of prophetic voices in North America, ICPL is an alliance where confirmed Prophets are able to relate to and connect with one another. We desire to be a safe environment for emerging prophetic voices to explore their gifting among seasoned leaders.

If you are a prophet, prophetic intercessor, or emerging prophetic voice, it is our desire that you would discover the valuable resources and relationships ICPL has to offer. You don't have to do ministry alone.

ICPL USA
P.O. BOX 4357 PENSACOLA FL, 32507
850.748.0895

ICPL CAN
P.O. Box 39 COPETOWN ON, L0R 1J0
905.308.9991

(f) @ICPLeaders // www.ICPLeaders.com

NEED PRAYER?

Eagle Worldwide Ministries, People Who Pray, is an apostolic prayer network comprised of intercessors from around the globe, providing prayer covering for not just our Network of Ministers and Ministries, but for anyone who is in need!

Need prayer? Email Us! Our team of prayer warriors is ready to pray for you.

Interested in becoming a part of People Who Pray as one of our intercessors? Email us!

EMAIL US:

PEOPLEWHOPRAY@EAGLEWORLDWIDE.COM

THE CENTRE FOR
EXCELLENCE
OF PENSACOLA

Impacting our community, one life at a time.

The Centre for Excellence is a US non-profit organization whose purpose is to offer practical resources, training, hope and support for individuals and families seeking to overcome a variety of life challenges including, but not limited to, poverty, addiction, and joblessness.

Visit the website below to see how you can join Dr. Russ in impacting lives by becoming a part of the Excellence Club today!

PROGRAMS & SERVICES

Food Distribution

Practical Skills Courses

Jamie's MOM'S HOUSE

Human Trafficking AWAREness

@Centre4Excellence.tdp

www.centre4excellence.com

Partner and Become a
KINGDOM ADVANCER
with Eagle Worldwide Ministries

$30 per month **$50** per month **$100** per month **$100+** per month

Do you want to see people impacted with the life-changing power of the Gospel? Do you believe in the priesthood of the believer and that each one of us has a mandate to be fruitful, multiply, and demonstrate the power and gifts of the Holy Spirit?

If you answered yes, then we would like to invite you to partner with Eagle Worldwide Ministries. As you partner together with Dr. Russ and Pastor Mave Moyer and the Eagle Worldwide Team, your financial seed will bear much Kingdom fruit. Won't you become a Kingdom Advancer with us today?

Start your monthly giving today!
visit www.eagleworldwide.com/become-a-partner

The King's Way Outreach Centre

Transforming our community, a *life* at a time.

The mission of The King's Way Outreach Centre is to provide practical resources, training opportunities and community outreach programs to those most vulnerable in our region. We empower individuals and families to overcome negative circumstances such as poverty, addiction and homelessness and help them achieve a better quality of life.

Visit the website below to see how you can make a difference and help those who need it the most.

Daily Food & Clothing Bank
Training & Support Programs
Holiday Hampers & Gifts
Toiletries & Hygiene Items

390 King William St, Hamilton ON L8L 1P6
905.296.9473 alifeatatime.com

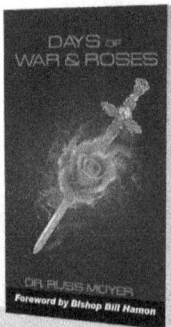

Author Contact Page

You may contact the author in the following ways:

By Email
bro.russ@eagleworldwide.com

By Phone:
+1 905 308 9991

By Mail:
PO Box 39
Copetown ON L0R1J0
Canada

On Facebook:

facebook.com/eagleworldwide

facebook.com/russ.moyer.52

By visiting his website:
www.EagleWorldwide.com